NANCY PELOSI

WHEN LITTLE NANCY PELOSI WAS JUST SEVEN YEARS OLD, A FRIEND OF THE FAMILY GAVE HER A STUFFED ELEPHANT.

NANCY *DIDN'T* LIKE IT.

EVEN THEN, NANCY KNEW.

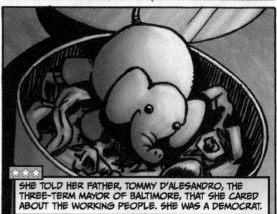

SHE TOLD HER FATHER, TOMMY D'ALESANDRO, THE THREE-TERM MAYOR OF BALTIMORE, THAT SHE CARED ABOUT THE WORKING PEOPLE. SHE WAS A DEMOCRAT.

I'M *SURE* 7-YEAR-OLD NANCY PELOSI CARED ABOUT THE *"WORKING PEOPLE."*

IT'S A GREAT WAY TO BEGIN HER STORY.

THAT'S AN URBAN LEGEND. NEVER HAPPENED.

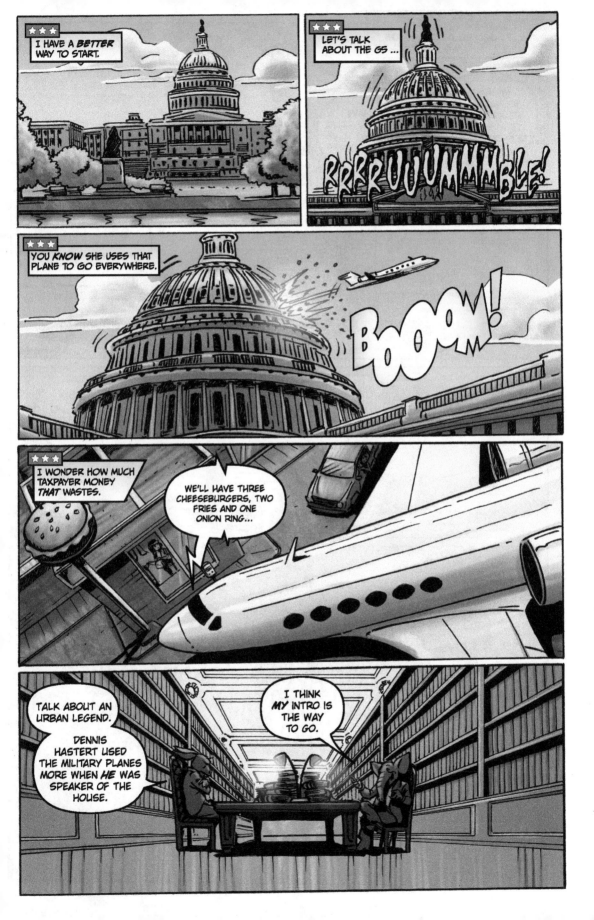

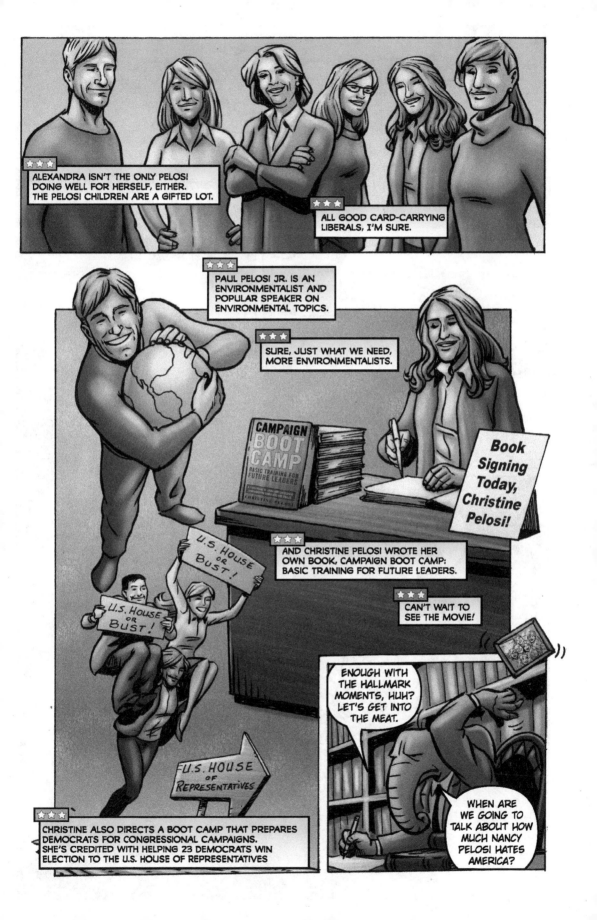

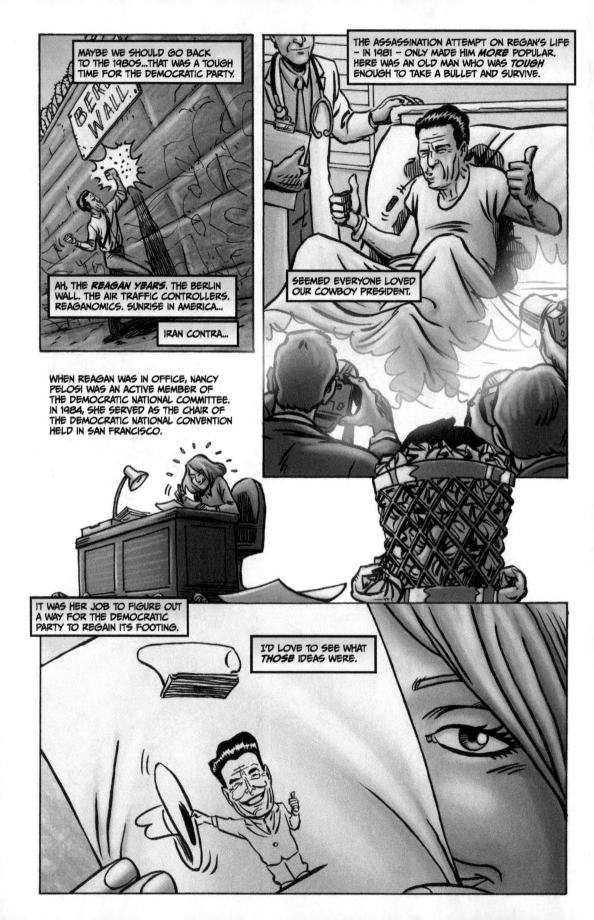

WHATEVER THEY WERE, THEY MUST HAVE MADE AN IMPACT. NANCY BECAME A RISING STAR IN THE DEMOCRATIC PARTY. CAMPAIGNING WAS IN HER *BLOOD*, PASSED ON FROM TOMMY THE ELDER, NO DOUBT. SHE WORKED HARD TO GET OTHER DEMOCRATS IN OFFICE.

IT WASN'T UNTIL 1987 THAT SOMEONE FINALLY CONVINCED NANCY THAT SHE SHOULD RUN FOR OFFICE *HERSELF*.

BEFORE SHE DIED IN EARLY 1987, SHE TOLD HER BROTHER-IN-LAW THAT NANCY SHOULD RUN FOR HER SEAT.

HER FRIEND, SALA BURTON, WAS A U.S. REPRESENTATIVE FROM SAN FRANCISCO. SHE WAS DYING FROM CANCER AND HAD ALREADY DECIDED NOT TO RUN FOR RE-ELECTION IN 1988.

THAT DECISION BY SALA BURTON WOULD EVENTUALLY CHANGE U.S. HISTORY.

IN 1987, THEN, NANCY PELOSI RAN HER FIRST CAMPAIGN FOR HERSELF, FIGHTING TO BECOME THE U.S. REPRESENTATIVE FROM THE 5TH CONGRESSIONAL DISTRICT OF CALIFORNIA.

HOW STRONG ARE WE IN THE FILMORE DISTRICT?

WE'RE LOOKING GOOD. *BRITT'S* PRETTY STRONG EVERYWHERE, TOO, THOUGH.

BRITT WAS *HARRY BRITT,* NANCY'S OPPONENT IN THAT FIRST RACE. HE WAS A DEMOCRAT *AND* A HOMOSEXUAL.

WOW. AND HE LOST THAT RACE HOW?

THE MOOD WAS TENSE THAT NIGHT AT PELOSI CAMPAIGN HEADQUARTERS.

NANCY PELOSI: A VOICE THAT WILL BE HEARD

THAT SLOGAN CERTAINLY TURNED OUT TO BE PROPHETIC. YOU CAN'T *NOT* HEAR THAT VOICE THESE DAYS.

NANCY PELOSI

NANCY WAS 46 WHEN SHE RAN THAT FIRST SUCCESSFUL CAMPAIGN, BEATING BRITT BY ABOUT 2,000 VOTES IN THE DEMOCRATIC PRIMARY.

THIS BEING SAN FRANCISCO, WINNING THE DEMOCRATIC PRIMARY WAS AS GOOD AS WINNING THAT CONGRESSIONAL SEAT. IN JUNE OF 1987, PELOSI EASILY BEAT REPUBLICAN CANDIDATE HARRIETT ROSS – GETTING 62 PERCENT OF THE VOTE – TO HEAD OFF TO THE HOUSE OF REPRESENTATIVES FOR THE FIRST TIME.

SEE THIS MATCH HEAD?

YEEEEES?

YOU COULD FIT A LIST OF NANCY PELOSI'S ACCOMPLISHMENTS WHILE IN OFFICE ON THIS MATCH HEAD...

AND STILL HAVE ROOM LEFT OVER FOR THE PHONE NUMBERS OF BILL CLINTON'S MISTRESSES.

YOU'RE WRONG ABOUT THAT, TRUNKS. NANCY HAS BEEN A PASSIONATE SUPPORTER OF AIDS RESEARCH AND FUNDING.

SHE'S PRESSURED CHINA ON ITS HISTORY OF HUMAN-RIGHTS VIOLATIONS.

AND SHE'S ADVANCED LEGISLATION TO PROTECT THE ENVIRONMENT.

AND FOR SOMEONE YOU CONSIDER A COMMUNIST, SHE'S BEEN VERY POPULAR WITH HER DISTRICT'S VOTERS.

Pelosi Wins – Again!

WHEN SHE RAN FOR HER FIRST FULL TERM IN 1988, SHE WON WITH 76 PERCENT OF THE VOTES.

LIKE I SAID EARLIER, WE JUST NEED A REALLY BIG SAW TO SLICE SAN FRANCISCO RIGHT OFF THE MAP.

WHEN THEY REWRITE THE HISTORY BOOKS, NANCY PELOSI DESERVES A HANDFUL OF CHAPTERS ALL FOR HERSELF.

U.S. HISTORY

YOU MEAN WE CAN DO THIS FOR *REAL*?

YES, GEORGE. *YES.* LIKE I'VE SAID... HUNDREDS OF TIMES.

⭐⭐⭐ NANCY WAS ONE OF THE STRONGEST VOICES IN OPPOSITION TO THE WAR IN IRAQ.

⭐⭐⭐ WE'VE ALWAYS KNOWN THAT PELOSI IS *UNPATRIOTIC*.

MISSION ACCOMPLISHED! MORE OR LESS.

⭐⭐⭐ IF THERE WERE MORE NANCY PELOSIS IN CONGRESS, HOW MANY FEWER DEAD SOLDIERS MIGHT WE HAVE RIGHT NOW?

DOES *THIS* COUNT?

⭐⭐⭐ AND JUST WHERE *ARE* THOSE WEAPONS OF MASS DESTRUCTION ANYWAY?

⭐⭐⭐ IT'S TOO BAD NOT *EVERY* INFLUENTIAL DEMOCRAT HAD THE FORESIGHT TO VOTE AGAINST THE WAR.

THERE IS *NO* EVIDENCE THAT IRAQ POSES A THREAT TO THE UNITED STATES!

⭐⭐⭐ IT'S TOO BAD HER VOICE WAS LARGELY DROWNED OUT.

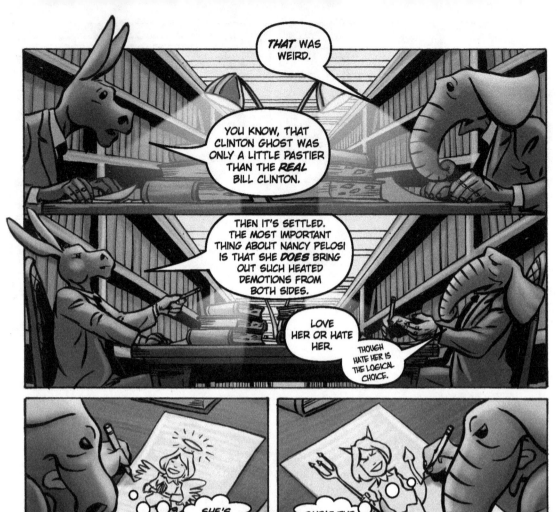

THE END

MICHELLE OBAMA

MICHELLE OBAMA: YEAR ONE

JANUARY 2009. THE INAUGURAL BALL IN WASHINGTON D.C. FIRST LADY MICHELLE OBAMA'S YEAR BEGINS IN HIGH STYLE.

ME? I'M HOME IN BROOKLYN, NEW YORK, WATCHING ON TELEVISION LIKE EVERYBODY ELSE.

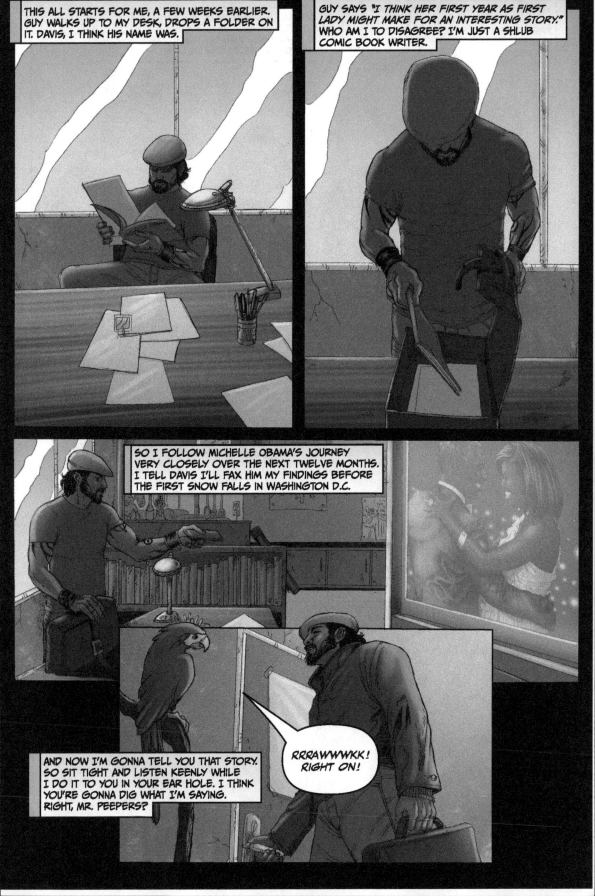

ON JANUARY 17TH, THREE DAYS BEFORE SHE WOULD OFFICIALLY BECOME FIRST LADY, MICHELLE CELEBRATED HER 45TH BIRTHDAY WITH HER HUSBAND AT THE EQUINOX, AN UPSCALE WASHINGTON D.C. RESTAURANT.

HOW DO I KNOW THIS? WHO DO YOU THINK WAS BUSING THEIR TABLE THAT EVENING?

MORE BREADSTICKS, MR. PRESIDENT-ELECT?

THAT DINNER WAS A NICE MOMENT—PROBABLY ONE OF THE LAST TRULY PRIVATE DINNERS EITHER OF THEM WILL HAVE FOR AT LEAST FOUR YEARS. THREE DAYS LATER, BARACK OBAMA WAS SWORN INTO OFFICE...AND EVERYTHING CHANGED.

IN AN EARLY SIGNAL THAT SHE WOULD NOT CONFINE HERSELF TO HOSTING TEAS AND REFEREEING AT EASTER EGG ROLLS, THE FIRST LADY WELCOMED LILLY LEDBETTER TO THE WHITE HOUSE TO COMMEMORATE THE SIGNING OF THE LANDMARK EQUAL PAY LEGISLATION NAMED IN HER HONOR.

THE FIRST DAYS OF A NEW ADMINISTRATION ARE ALL ABOUT LAYING DOWN MARKERS. IN MICHELLE OBAMA'S CASE, STAKING OUT A ZONE OF PRIVACY FOR HER DAUGHTERS WAS OF PARAMOUNT IMPORTANCE.

WHEN A PROMINENT U.S. TOYMAKER TRIED TO MARKET "BEANIE" STYLE DOLLS NAMED "SWEET SASHA" AND "MARVELOUS MALIA," THE NEW FIRST MOM HIT THE CEILING.

"WE BELIEVE IT IS INAPPROPRIATE TO USE YOUNG PRIVATE CITIZENS FOR MARKETING PURPOSES," SHE SAID THROUGH A SPOKESWOMAN. AND THE DOLLS WERE IMMEDIATELY TAKEN OFF THE MARKET.

DETERMINED NOT TO BE PIGEONHOLED—AS PREVIOUS FIRST LADIES HAD—AS AMERICA'S STYLISTA-IN-CHIEF, MICHELLE ALSO CARVED OUT A ROLE FOR HERSELF IN THE AREA OF PUBLIC POLICY.

SHE SPOKE OUT EARLY AND OFTEN ON BEHALF OF HER HUSBAND'S STIMULUS PACKAGE, DESIGNED TO JUMPSTART THE AILING ECONOMY.

LIKE THE LILY LEDBETTER RECEPTION, THOSE APPEARANCES RECEIVED SCANT COVERAGE IN THE PRESS, WHICH SEEMED UNNATURALLY OBSESSED WITH THE NEW FIRST LADY'S WELL-TONED ARMS.

ADMITTEDLY, THAT FIRST OFFICIAL WHITE HOUSE PORTRAIT DIDN'T HELP. WELCOME TO THE GUN SHOW, AMERICA!

LIKEWISE, A FEBRUARY SPEECH ON GLOBAL WARMING IN FRONT OF AN AUDIENCE OF 1000 AT THE ENVIRONMENTAL PROTECTION AGENCY...

...WAS DROWNED OUT BY THE CACOPHONY SURROUNDING THE UNVEILING OF A MICHELLE OBAMA WAX DUMMY AT MADAME TUSSAUD'S IN WASHINGTON D.C.

IF THERE WERE PITFALLS TO BEING AN INTERNATIONAL CELEBRITY, THERE WERE PERKS AS WELL. IN APRIL, MICHELLE MADE HER FIRST TRIP ABROAD AS FIRST LADY.

THE EUROPEAN TOUR WAS A MIX OF STYLE, SUBSTANCE... AND SLAPSTICK. IN ENGLAND, SHE VISITED A CANCER WARD WITH THE WIFE OF BRITISH PRIME MINISTER GORDON BROWN.

IT WAS A GOOD PHOTO OP—AND IT HELPED WIN OVER THE USUALLY SNARKY BRITISH TABLOIDS TO HER SIDE. ONE NEWSPAPER ACCOUNT CRACKED THAT, NEXT TO AMERICA'S FIRST LADY, SARAH BROWN LOOKED *"ABOUT AS EXCITING AS A BOWL OF CORN FLAKES."*

I GOT A GOOD CHUCKLE OUT OF THAT ONE-CEREAL CONNOISSEUR THAT I AM.

THEN THERE WAS A BIT OF A KERFUFFLE IN THE PRESS WHEN MICHELLE BREACHED ROYAL ETIQUETTE BY TOUCHING QUEEN ELIZABETH'S BACK DURING A RECEPTION AT BUCKINGHAM PALACE.

UNDETERRED BY THE NAYSAYERS, MRS. O PRESSED ON WITH HER GARDEN. SHE EVEN WENT ON SESAME STREET TO SING THE PRAISES OF LOCALLY GROWN ORGANIC VEGETABLES.

ELMO WASN'T THE ONLY ADORABLE FURRY CREATURE TO MEET THE FIRST LADY THAT SPRING. THE EASTER BUNNY HIMSELF DROPPED BY THE WHITE HOUSE FOR THE ANNUAL ROLLING OF THE EGGS.

YOU CYNICS OUT THERE CAN CHUCKLE ALL YOU WANT, BUT THE KIDS DUG IT AND THE FIRST LADY USED THE EVENT TO PROMOTE THE IDEA OF PHYSICAL FITNESS AND COMBATING OBESITY.

MY HOMEGIRL FERGIE EVEN ROCKED THE HOUSE WITH A SONG. HOW DO I KNOW THIS? I WAS THERE WITH MY KID.

WHAT DO YOU THINK? I'M MADE OF WOOD OR SOMETHING?

SORRY, HATERS, BUT THERE WERE MORE TRIPS TO COME AS SPRING GAVE WAY TO SUMMER. LIKE MOST AMERICAN FAMILIES, THE FIRST FAMILY SCHEDULED THEIR VACATIONS AROUND THE KIDS' SCHOOL SCHEDULES.

THE OBAMAS' EXCELLENT ADVENTURE BEGAN OUT WEST, WHERE THEY TOOK IN THE SIGHTS AT AMERICA'S NATIONAL PARKS. THEY GOT TO WATCH OLD FAITHFUL BLOW HIS STACK.

AND THEY TOOK IN THE MAJESTIC GRAND CANYON.

NATURALLY THERE HAD TO BE SOME KIND OF MEDIA-GENERATED HOO-HA ABOUT MICHELLE'S APPEARANCE. THIS TIME IT WAS ALL ABOUT HER SHORTS—AND WHETHER IT WAS APPROPRIATE FOR HER TO BE SHOWING SO MUCH LEG IN THE 120-DEGREE ARIZONA HEAT.

ME, I GET AROUND THAT PROBLEM BY LIVING A FULL-ON NUDIST LIFESTYLE THROUGHOUT THE WARM WEATHER MONTHS. BUT MAYBE I SHOULD SPARE YOU THAT PANEL.

IN ANY CASE, I MISSED THE WESTERN SWING DUE TO AIRPORT REGULATIONS ON PERSONAL HYGIENE. BUT I WAS FULLY CLOTHED AND BACK ON THE CASE WHEN THE OBAMAS MADE THEIR NEXT STOP, ON MARTHA'S VINEYARD.

NICE PLACE, THE VINEYARD. JAMES TAYLOR AND I HAVE A HOUSE UP THERE. FOR THE FIRST FAMILY, IT WAS A CHANCE TO DO SOME SLUMMING, EAT CRUMMY TAKEOUT FOOD LIKE THE REST OF US FOR A CHANGE.

THERE WAS THE OBLIGATORY FAMILY BIKE RIDE PHOTO OP.

AND A VISIT TO ONE OF THOSE "OLD TIMEY" CANDY STORES YOUR GRANDPA'S ALWAYS BANGING ON ABOUT.

UNFORTUNATELY, SUMMER VACATION WRAPPED UP ON A SAD NOTE WITH NEWS OF THE PASSING OF SENATOR EDWARD KENNEDY, ONE OF BARACK OBAMA'S POLITICAL PADRONES.

THE FIRST COUPLE HEADED TO MASSACHUSETTS FOR THE FUNERAL.

ATTENDING FUNERALS IS ONE OF THE LEAST GLAMOROUS, MOST UNHERALDED ASPECTS OF BEING FIRST LADY. YOU DON'T READ ABOUT THIS PART OF THE GIG IN THE STYLE PAGES, BUT IT'S ABSOLUTELY NECESSARY. YOU TAKE THE CRUNCHY WITH THE SMOOTH, I GUESS.

A SEPTEMBER WING DING HELD IN HONOR OF WORLD SPACE WEEK BROUGHT 150 SCHOOL KIDS TO THE WHITE HOUSE SOUTH LAWN FOR AN EVENING OF STAR GAZING.

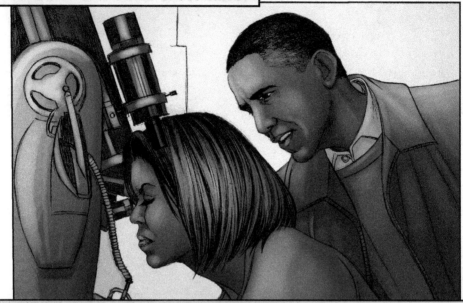

ALL THAT SCHMOOZING WITH THE LITTLE ONES MUST HAVE PAID OFF, AS THE FIRST LADY WAS NAMED THE HONORARY NATIONAL PRESIDENT OF THE GIRL SCOUTS OF THE USA. AS A FORMER SCOUT MYSELF, I CAN REPORT THERE IS NO HIGHER HONOR THAN THIS.

BACK IN THE LAND OF GROWN-UPS, MICHELLE WORKED WITH AMERICA'S MUSEUM CURATORS ON A SELECTION OF 45 PIECES OF ART TO HANG ON THE WALLS OF THE WHITE HOUSE PRIVATE RESIDENCE AND OFFICES.

SHE MADE SOME BOLD CHOICES. NOT THIS *BOLD*, THOUGH. A PORTRAIT OF THE PRESIDENT WITH A SLICE OF COCONUT CREAM PIE ON HIS HEAD DID NOT MAKE THE CUT.

SPEAKING OF PASTRY....ENTERTAINING CONTINUED TO TAKE UP A LOT OF THE FIRST LADY'S TIME. IN SEPTEMBER, SHE HAD DUTCH CROWN PRINCE WILLEM-ALEXANDER AND PRINCESS MAXIMA OVER FOR TEA.

FOLLOWING HER LEAD ON THE HEALTHY EATING FRONT, A LOCAL WASHINGTON D.C. EATERY INTRODUCED THE MICHELLE MELT, A TURKEY BURGER MADE WITH FRESH, LOCALLY GROWN INGREDIENTS.

THE FIRST LADY TRIED ONE HERSELF AND PRONOUNCED IT GOOD EATING. LOCAVORE THAT I AM, I'M INCLINED TO AGREE.

ONE PRESUMES THE GRUB WASN'T QUITE AS NOURISHING LATER IN OCTOBER, WHEN MICHELLE AND VICE PRESIDENT BIDEN'S WIFE JILL ATTENDED GAME ONE OF THE WORLD SERIES AT YANKEE STADIUM.

YOGI BERRA WAS ON HAND—AND SO WAS I.

SOMEWHERE IN THAT WHIRLWIND OF ACTIVITY THE OBAMAS FOUND TIME TO CELEBRATE THEIR CELEBRATING THEIR SEVENTEENTH WEDDING ANNIVERSARY AT THE BLUEDUCK TAVERN, A SOIGNÉE RESTAURANT IN THE NATION'S CAPITAL.

LIFE WASN'T ALL TEA CAKES AND TURKEY BURGERS, OF COURSE. THERE WAS STILL IMPORTANT WORK TO BE DONE.

IN OCTOBER, THE FIRST LADY JOURNEYED TO COPENHAGEN TO LEND SUPPORT TO THE CITY OF CHICAGO'S BID TO HOST THE 2016 SUMMER OLYMPICS.

SHE MET WITH INTERNATIONAL OLYMPIC COMMITTEE PRESIDENT JACQUES ROGGE AND PRESSED HER HOMETOWN'S CASE AT A SERIES OF HIGH-PROFILE SCHMOOZEFESTS.

IN THE END, SADLY, IT WAS NOT TO BE. CHICAGO CAME IN FOURTH OF THE FOUR FINALISTS MAKING THEIR PITCHES IN THE DANISH CAPITAL. CHICAGOANS WERE CRUSHED. IT WAS A RARE MOMENT OF DISAPPOINTMENT IN AN OTHERWISE SUCCESSFUL YEAR FOR THE FIRST LADY.

AFTER THE STING OF THE OLYMPIC REJECTION WORE OFF, MICHELLE RETURNED TO OTHER IMPORTANT BUSINESS. UNFORTUNATELY, THE MEDIA REMAINED OBSESSED WITH TRIVIALITIES.

THE FIRST LADY GAVE A SPEECH ON WOMEN AND HEALTH CARE AT THE EISENHOWER EXECUTIVE OFFICE BUILDING IN WASHINGTON. BUT ALL THE PRESS WANTED TO TALK ABOUT WAS THE LARGE BELT SHE WORE FOR THE OCCASION.

ADMITTEDLY, MICHELLE ALSO EXPLOITED HER CELEBRITY CACHET WHEN IT SUITED HER PURPOSES. SHE USED THE FORUM OF A PRIME TIME JAY LENO SHOW APPEARANCE IN OCTOBER TO RENEW HER CALL FOR AMERICANS TO SUPPORT MILITARY FAMILIES.

IT'S A FINE LINE YOU HAVE TO WALK: CALL ATTENTION TO IMPORTANT CAUSES--AND BE ABLE TO PULL OFF HOSTING THE WHITE HOUSE HALLOWEEN PARTY.

I THOUGHT THE FIRST LADY MADE A FINE CATWOMAN, BY THE WAY. ME, I WENT AS RA'AS AL-GHUL.

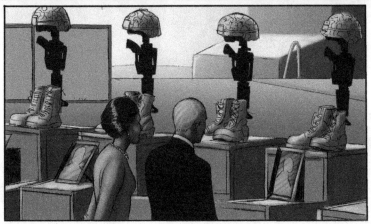

AND WHEN TRAUMATIC REAL-LIFE EVENTS INTERVENE--LIKE THE FUNERALS OF SLAIN SOLDIERS AT FORT HOOD--WELL, YOU HAVE TO SWITCH GEARS AND HANDLE THAT TOO.

THE REST OF MICHELLE'S YEAR WAS SPENT DOING THE USUAL MUNDANE HOLIDAY TASKS WE ALL DO, LIKE, UH, GREETING THE VICTORIAN COACHMAN WHO HAND DELIVERS YOUR ENORMOUS BESPOKE CHRISTMAS TREE.

WAIT...DID I SAY CHRISTMAS? ODDS BODKINS, I'VE GET TO FAX MY REPORT OFF TO BLUEWATER WORLD HEADQUARTERS TOUT DE SUITE!

SORRY, KIDS, GOTTA BUG!

WHEW! JUST IN TIME!

AND STILL TWO PAGES LEFT TO TIE THINGS UP WITH A NICE, TIDY BOW!

AND ON THAT NOTE, OUR YEAR IN THE LIFE OF MICHELLE OBAMA COMES TO AN END. BUT DON'T WORRY. WITH THREE YEARS TO GO IN BARACK'S FIRST TERM, THIS IS REALLY ONLY THE BEGINNING OF THE STORY.

WHY, IF THIS WERE A SUPERHERO COMIC BOOK, WE'D HAVE JUST GOTTEN THROUGH THE ORIGIN STORY AND THE HERO'S FIRST ADVENTURE.

MICHELLE OBAMA WOULD JUST BE LEARNING THE FULL EXTENT OF HER POWERS, MAKING SMALL ALTERATIONS TO HER COSTUME, AND GETTING READY TO TAKE ON HER FIRST SUPERVILLAIN.

BUT WHILE SHE'S AN EXTRAORDINARY WOMAN IN MANY RESPECTS, MICHELLE OBAMA IS NOT A SUPERHERO. NOT YET ANYWAY. BUT WHO KNOWS?

ONE LITTLE BUG BITE AND SHE COULD BE CRAWLING THE WHITE HOUSE WALLS AND SLINGING WEBS AT JOE BIDEN.

WHO KNOWS? MAYBE I'LL EVEN BE THERE TO SEE THAT. MAKE A FEW BUCKS SELLING THE PICTURES TO THE PAPERS.

MORNING, MRS. O!

OH, UH, GOOD MORNING, CHICHESTER.

CONDOLEEZZA RICE

CON DOCEZZA! CONNN DOCEZZA!

THE STORY GOES THAT CONDI'S MOTHER, AN OPERA FAN, NAMED HER FOR THE ITALIAN MUSICAL NOTATION "CON DOCEZZA"-- OR "WITH SWEETNESS." HER NAME IS UNUSUAL NOW, MORE SO IN 1954.

ALABAMA, 1892

OTHERS POINT TO A MORE HISTORICALLY COMPLEX ORIGIN FOR HER NAME: HER SLAVERY ROOTS.

HER GRANDPARENTS WERE PLANTATION SLAVES, SOME "FAVORED" HOUSE SERVANTS WHO RECEIVED EDUCATION. AN ITALIAN MAN NAMED ALTO-- CONDI'S GREAT-GREAT-GRANDFATHER-- FATHERED CHILDREN WITH THEM.

BUT, FOR SOME REASON, ITALIAN NAMES CONTINUED IN RICE'S LINEAGE FOR GENERATIONS AFTER, DESPITE THE TOUCHY NATURE OF THEIR BIRTHRIGHT.

WE HAVE A RACIAL BIRTH DEFECT THAT WE'VE NEVER QUITE DEALT WITH... WE ARE MORE INTERTWINED AND INTERTANGLED THAN WE WOULD LIKE TO THINK.

IT'S A LEGACY THAT WAS BASICALLY NOT ONE OF CHOICE AND VOLITION BUT OF VIOLENCE AND OPPRESSION... AND SO I THINK THAT'S WHY PEOPLE HAVE TROUBLE ADMITTING IT AND TALKING ABOUT IT AND UNDERSTANDING IT.

THE VULCAN IS ALSO A MAJOR PART OF CONDOLEEZZA'S UPBRINGING.

I DON'T THINK THIS IS LOGICAL-- YOU MUST BE THINKING OF A DIFFERENT VULCAN. PERHAPS THE FAMOUS STATUE IN BIRMINGHAM, ALABAMA, WHERE CONDOLEEZZA WAS BORN?

UMM... RIGHT. SHOULD HAVE RESEARCHED MORE. THANKS, SPOCK.

A PLEASURE TO BE OF ASSISTANCE. NOW, AS THEY SAY, "10-4, GOOD BUDDY."

BIRMINGHAM WAS ONCE KNOWN AS "THE MAGIC CITY," A THRIVING POST-CIVIL WAR STEEL TOWN. THE ROMAN GOD OF FIRE, VULCAN, WATCHED OVER IN THE FORM OF THE WORLD'S LARGEST STEEL SCULPTURE.

CONDI'S GRANDFATHER SETTLED HERE IN 1904 WITH DROVES OF HOPEFUL BLACK WORKERS, LOOKING TO MAKE THEIR WAY AT THE TURN OF THE CENTURY.

SOMEDAY, CONDI'S FOREIGN POLICY TEAM WOULD EVEN BE DUBBED "THE VULCANS" AFTER THE STATUE-- A SYMBOL OF INSPIRATION AND POWER.

BUT BY THE TIME CONDOLEEZZA WAS BORN IN 1954, HER ONCE-STRONG CITY HAD EARNED A NEW NICKNAME...

"THE YEAR 1963 IN BIRMINGHAM SHATTERED CONDOLEEZZA RICE'S COMFORTABLE COCOON."
-ELISABETH BUMILLER, BIOGRAPHER

JOCKEY BOY RESTAURANT

101

THE KU KLUX KLAN, BOMBINGS, BLOODSHED-- IT SEEMS STRANGE TO THINK SOME BLACKS DID NOT WANT A PREACHER NAMED MARTIN LUTHER KING COMING TO BIRMINGHAM TO PROTEST.

MIDDLE-CLASS BLACKS LIKE THE RICE'S WERE SEGREGATED, BUT ADMITTEDLY COMFORTABLE. ONCE KING ROCKED THE BOAT, THERE WOULD BE NO GOING BACK. THEY KNEW THE COST.

SOME OF THE PEOPLE SITTING HERE TODAY WILL NOT COME BACK ALIVE FROM THIS CAMPAIGN.

BAN RACISM FOREVER

STOP RACISM

WE SHALL OVERCOME

KNOWING WHAT HE KNEW ABOUT MAN'S CAPACITY TO HATE, KING CONTROVERSIALLY CALLED BIRMINGHAM'S CHILDREN TO RALLY AND MARCH.

AT 100 FEET, THEIR HOSES COULD KNOCK BRICKS LOOSE FROM A WALL.

BUT AT POINT BLANK RANGE... THE EFFECT IS TOO AWFUL TO IMAGINE

THE PROBLEM IS, THOUGH CONDI WAS A GOOD PIANO PLAYER, MANY YOUNGER STUDENTS COULD PLAY IN MINUTES WHAT IT TOOK HER YEARS TO LEARN. SHE HAD AN EPIPHANY: "CONCERT PIANIST" WAS NOT A FEASIBLE CAREER.

WOW.

THE DREAM SHE'D HAD SINCE AGE THREE WAS SUDDENLY SHATTERED. AND SHE'D NEVER SETTLE FOR JUST TEACHING PIANO.

AND SINCE THEY'D ALREADY BOUGHT HER A $13,000 GRAND PIANO, CONDI'S PARENTS WERE VERY ILL-PLEASED WITH HER CHANGE OF HEART.

WHAT ARE YOU GOING TO DO WITH YOUR LIFE THEN? WAITRESS?

I'D RATHER WAITRESS THAN TEACH PIANO! AND SO WHAT IF I DO? IT'S MY LIFE!

WELL, IT'S OUR MONEY. PICK A NEW CAREER. AND QUICK.

NOT TO BE FLIPPANT, BUT CONDOLEEZZA FELL INTO INTERNATIONAL POLITICS THE WAY PEOPLE PICK BINGO NUMBERS-- TOTALLY BY CHANCE.

WHEEL OF CAREERS

CATTLE RUSTLER
AUTO REPAIR
BEAVER TRAPPER
INTERNATIONAL POLITICS
UMPIRE
INVENT THE INTERNET
BASIC CABLE
CLIP SHOW HOST
HIGH SCHOOL TEACHER
SECRETARY OF STATE
LITERARY AGENT
ANIMAL HUSH...
FITNESS TRAINER
DENTAL HYGIENIST

BUT THE RIGHT PERSON, THE RIGHT TEACHER, CAN SHAPE YOUR ENTIRE LIFE. AND SO IT WAS FOR CONDOLEEZZA, AND HER MENTOR, JOSEF KORBEL.

A RESPECTED AND INFLUENTIAL EXPERT ON SOVIET POLITICS, KORBEL COINCIDENTALLY WAS ALSO FATHER TO MADELEINE ALBRIGHT, THE FUTURE FIRST WOMAN SECRETARY OF STATE.

A QUICK WORD IS IN ORDER ABOUT CONDOLEEZZA'S POLITICAL AFFILIATIONS. I KNOW, I KNOW... *YAWN*. STICK WITH ME HERE, FOLKS.

CONDI VOLUNTEERED FOR DEMOCRAT GARY HART'S CAMPAIGN IN 1980, BUT THEN VOTED FOR REPUBLICAN SUPERSTAR RONALD REAGAN IN THE NEXT PRESIDENTIAL ELECTION. REAGAN'S DEMOCRATIC OPPONENT, JIMMY CARTER, MAY HAVE BEEN A FELLOW SOUTHERNER, BUT SHE HAD PROBLEMS WITH THE WAY HE WOULD HANDLE THE SOVIETS.

THE OTHER REASON FOR CONDI'S REPUBLICAN ALLEGIANCE? IN 1952, CONDI'S FATHER TRIED TO VOTE DEMOCRATIC AND WAS SUBJECTED TO A BOGUS "POLL TEST," AND TOLD IF HE FAILED THE TEST, HE COULDN'T VOTE.

RICE, JOHN. HERE TO REGISTER AS A DEMOCRA--

NOT SO FAST. FIRST YOU GOTTA GUESS HOW MANY JELLY BEANS ARE IN THIS JAR.

...

AWW, C'MON... CAN'T I JUST *HAVE* ONE?

OH GEE MISTER, COME RIGHT IN, COME RIGHT IN!

WELCOME TO THE REPUBLICAN PARTY! CAN I GET YOU *ANYTHING?* HAVE YOU EATEN? WE HAVE LOTS OF JELLY BEANS, MAN THEY'RE *GOOD!*

REPUBLIC PARTY

THIS WAS AN ACTUAL METHOD USED TO KEEP BLACKS OUT OF VOTING BOOTHS. I *SWEAR* IT'S TRUE.

BUT, ACROSS TOWN, THE *REPUBLICANS* WERE LOSING MEMBERS AND TAKING *ANYBODY* IN. JOHN RICE WAS A LOYAL REPUBLICAN FROM THAT DAY ON AND, EVENTUALLY, HIS DAUGHTER FOLLOWED SUIT.

1981

AFTER CONDI'S TEACHER, JOSEF KORBEL PASSED AWAY, SHE WAS CRUSHED. BUT SHE VOWED TO MAKE HIM PROUD, AND CONTINUED HER EDUCATION WITH AN EYE TOWARDS MILITARY INTELLIGENCE, WHICH NOW FASCINATED HER.

MADE UP MY MIND TO MAKE A NEW START, GOING TO CALIFORNIA WITH AN ACHING IN MY HEART...

AND SHE WOULD DO IT FROM THE PRESTIGIOUS STANFORD UNIVERSITY.

MEET THE BUSHES!

1991

President George HW Bush

First Lady Barbara Bush

Future President George W. Bush

Millie, First Dog

...ANOTHER WAR WAS BEGINNING.

CONDI'S LIFE WOULD CHANGE FOREVER IN 1988, AFTER MEETING A NICE TEXAS FAMILY.

SHE TELLS ME EVERYTHING I KNOW ABOUT THE SOVIET UNION.

PLUS, I'VE SEEN "ROCKY 4" EIGHT TIMES.

BUT IRAQ WOULDN'T BE CONDI'S HEADACHE. NOT YET, ANYWAY.

AT STANFORD, CONDI CAUGHT THE EYE OF THE PRESIDENT, AND BECAME HIS NATIONAL SECURITY ADVISOR-- AN ENORMOUS RESPONSIBILITY.

THOUGH YOUNG, CONDI QUICKLY GAINED A REPUTATION FOR BEING DIPLOMATIC, INTELLIGENT... AND TOUGH AS NAILS.

WE'RE HERE, MR. YELTSIN. FOR SECURITY REASONS, WE'LL ENTER THE *WHITE HOUSE* THROUGH THE BACK...

A *SERVICE* ENTRANCE?! DO YOU KNOW WHO I AM? I'M NOT GETTING OUT OF THE CAR FOR THIS.

...LIKE WHEN SHE LITERALLY DRUG A STUBBORN BORIS YELTSIN UP A FLIGHT OF STAIRS, IRONICALLY, INTO A DIPLOMACY MEETING.

YOU KNOW... FOR THE *GREATER GOOD*.

RIGHT THIS WAY, SIR. I *INSIST*.

RICE'S HARD WORK WAS AN IMPORTANT PART OF THE *REUNIFICATION OF SOCIALIST EAST AND DEMOCRATIC WEST GERMANY* AS ONE FREE COUNTRY.

NOT TO MENTION, MAKING SURE THE SOVIETS DIDN'T FEEL THREATENED, LOSE THEIR COOL AND LAUNCH NUCLEAR WARHEADS.

BUT AS THE COLD WAR WAS ENDING...

SHE WAS HEADED BACK TO STANFORD TO TEACH AGAIN, AND WOULD EVEN BECOME PROVOST OF THE ENTIRE SCHOOL-- THE FIRST BLACK WOMAN, AND YOUNGEST PERSON, TO EVER DO SO.

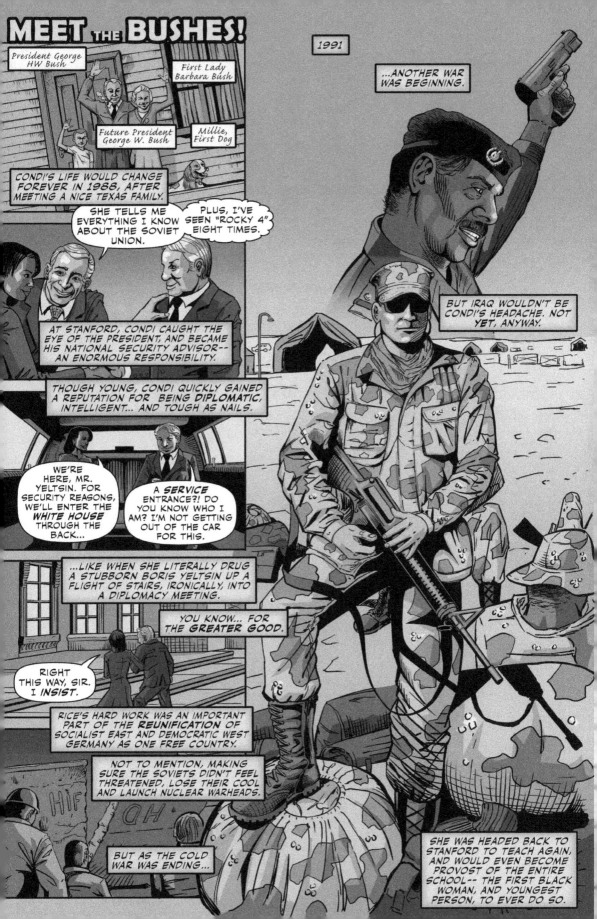

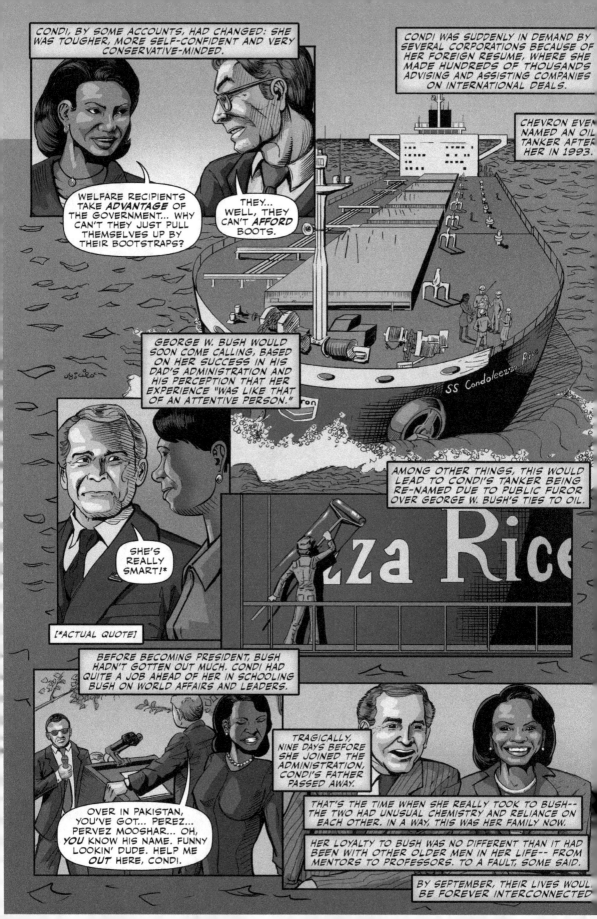

THE WAR IN IRAQ.

IT'S THE REASON YOU KNOW *CONDOLEEZZA RICE'S* NAME.

IT'S DEFINITELY THE REASON SOME PEOPLE WON'T GO *NEAR* THIS COMIC BOOK.

THE TERM "DIVISIVE WAR" IS AN UNDERSTATEMENT.

WHATEVER YOU BELIEVE, HERE ARE SOME *FACTS*:

THE US DID NOT FIND WEAPONS OF MASS DESTRUCTION IN IRAQ-- THE INTELLIGENCE WAS PROVEN FAULTY.

THE US WAS NOT IMMEDIATELY GREETED AS LIBERATORS, AS DONALD RUMSFELD ONCE PRESUPPOSED.

POST-SADDAM IRAQ COLLAPSED INTO CIVIL WAR AND CHAOS, WITH NO EXIT IN SIGHT.

AND BY THE TIME CONDI WAS OFFERED THE SECRETARY OF STATE POSITION IN BUSH'S SECOND TERM, THE TIDE OF PUBLIC OPINION TURNED ON CONDOLEEZZA AND HER BOSS.

WE DON'T WANT THE *SMOKING GUN* TO BE A MUSHROOM CLOUD.

1988

RICE'S COLLEAGUES WERE SURPRISED TO SEE THE "CAREFUL DIPLOMACY" SHE EXHIBITED IN PRESIDENT GEORGE HW BUSH'S CABINET TURN INTO HAWK-LIKE ATTITUDES ABOUT WAR IN GEORGE W.'S SERVICE.

SOME SUGGEST SHE WAS ILL-PREPARED FOR THE MONUMENTAL TASK OF A NEW KIND OF WAR, WITH A NEW KIND OF ENEMY. THE TERRORISTS MADE HARD-LINE SOVIETS LOOK TAME.

BRENT SCOWCROFT, WHO LAUNCHED CONDI'S POLITICAL CAREER BY OFFERING HER A JOB IN GEORGE HW BUSH'S CABINET IN 1988, NOW CLASHED WITH HER OVER IRAQ, CALLING HER OUT IN MUCH-PUBLICIZED EDITORIAL TITLED "DON'T ATTACK SADDAM."

"I DON'T UNDERSTAND HOW MY LADY, MY BABE MY DISCIPLE, HAS CHANGED SO MUCH," HE LATER SAID.

IT'S ALL VERY SHAKESPEARIAN SOUNDING. OR GEORGE LUCAS-ISH, I SUPPOSE. EVEN CONDI'S STEPMOTHER CLARA IN BIRMINGHAM CONFESSED TO CONDI THAT SHE THOUGHT BIN LADEN WAS WHO THEY WERE AFTER... NOT SADDAM.

I'LL GIVE HER THIS: HAD CONDI BEEN SECRETARY OF STATE IN OBAMA'S CABINET, INSTEAD OF HILLARY CLINTON, RUSSIAN RELATIONS WOULD BE LESS EMBARRASSING.

THE BUTTON IS SYMBOLIC, 'PEREGRUZKA' MEANS 'RESET'! SEE?

[ACTUALLY, IT MEANS 'OVERCHARGE.' THANKS FOR PLAYING, CHAMP.]

*TRANSLATED FROM RUSSIAN

BUT HER RUSSIAN EXPERTISE WAS TRUMPED BY IRAQ.

HAVE YOU EVER TRIED TO SHOVEL A SIDEWALK WHILE IT'S STILL SNOWING? THIS MIGHT SUM UP CONDI'S WELL-MEANING, BUT ULTIMATELY FAILED, EFFORTS TO STABILIZE IRAQ AND HEAL WOUNDS WITH US ENEMIES AND ALLIES.

THE CONSTANT HEAD-BUTTING WITH RUMSFELD, CHENEY AND UNCOOPERATIVE GOVERNMENTAL AGENCIES PROBABLY DIDN'T HELP, EITHER.

RICE NEEDED A GOOD PUBLICITY MANAGER. EVEN SOMETHING AS INNOCENT AS THE CHANCE TO PLAY ALONGSIDE HER HERO YO-YO MA APPEARED TO MANY AS NERO FIDDLING WHILE ROME BURNED.

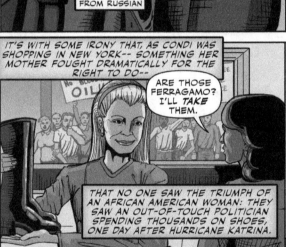

IT'S WITH SOME IRONY THAT, AS CONDI WAS SHOPPING IN NEW YORK-- SOMETHING HER MOTHER FOUGHT DRAMATICALLY FOR THE RIGHT TO DO--

ARE THOSE FERRAGAMO? I'LL TAKE THEM.

THAT NO ONE SAW THE TRIUMPH OF AN AFRICAN AMERICAN WOMAN: THEY SAW AN OUT-OF-TOUCH POLITICIAN SPENDING THOUSANDS ON SHOES, ONE DAY AFTER HURRICANE KATRINA.

NO BLOOD FOR OIL!!!

WHEN THE LEVEE BREAKS I'LL HAVE NO PLACE TO STAY

IRAQ BLOOD ON YOUR HANDS!

SECURITY! GET THOSE PEOPLE AWAY FROM THIS STORE! I'M SORRY, MS. RICE... LET ME WRAP THESE FOR YOU.

SONIA SOTOMAYOR

JULY 13, 2009. SONIA MARIA SOTOMAYOR RAISES HER RIGHT HAND TO BE SWORN IN BEFORE THE U.S. SENATE JUDICIARY COMMITTEE.

SHE WILL ENDURE FOUR GRUELING DAYS OF HEARINGS.

WHEN THE SMOKE CLEARS, SHE WILL HAVE WON CONFIRMATION TO THE LIFETIME APPOINTMENT BY A 68-31 MARGIN. IN THE SPACE OF A FEW WEEKS, SHE WILL HAVE BECOME ONE OF THE MOST POWERFUL WOMEN IN AMERICA.

AND WHEN THE COURT RECONVENE IN SEPTEMBER, SHE WILL SLIP ON HER BLACK ROBES TAKE HER PLACE ALONG SIDE THE OTHER MEMBERS OF AMERICA'S MOST AUGUST JUDICIAL BODY.

BUT AFTER ALL THAT SCRUTINY, HOW WELL WILL WE REALLY KNOW HER? CAN WE TRUST HER TO RULE JUSTLY AND FAIRLY ON THE CONSTITUTIONAL ISSUES THAT AFFECT ALL OUR LIVES?

JUST WHO IS THIS WOMAN AND HOW DID SHE COME TO BE INVESTED WITH SUCH POWER?

HI. I'M ROBERT SCHNAKENBERG—WRITER, RACONTEUR, AND C-SPAN JUNKIE.

YOU MAY REMEMBER ME FROM SUCH COMIC BOOK BIOGRAPHIES AS *FEMALE FORCE: BARBARA WALTERS.*

I'M ALSO THE AUTHOR OF A BOOK CALLED *SECRET LIVES OF THE SUPREME COURT.*

YOU MIGHT THINK THAT WOULD MAKE ME AN EXPERT ON THE LIFE AND CAREER OF JUSTICE SONIA SOTOMAYOR.

BUT NO— I'M LEARNING ALL ABOUT HER ALONG WITH THE REST OF AMERICA.

AND I GOTTA TELL YA: I'M INTRIGUED BY WHAT I SEE SO FAR. NO MATTER YOUR POLITICAL PERSUASION THIS IS ONE IMPRESSIVE LADY.

PRINCETON EDUCATED, YALE LAW SCHOOL GRAD, WORKED IN THE ROUGH-AND-TUMBLE MANHATTAN DISTRICT ATTORNEY'S OFFICE.

YESSIR, SHE'S SEEN AND DONE A LOT IN HER 55 YEARS ON THIS BIG BLUE MARBLE WE CALL HOME.

YOU MIGHT EVEN CALL HER A *"WISE LATINA."*

JUSTICE SOTOMAYOR'S STORY BEGINS, AS ALL GREAT STORIES DO, IN A PUBLIC HOSPITAL IN THE BRONX, ON JUNE 25, 1954. IT WAS A VERY HOT AND HUMID DAY. TRUST ME. I LOOKED IT UP.

MATERNITY

SONIA'S FIRST HOME WAS A TINY TENEMENT IN THE SOUTH BRONX. HER FATHER, JUAN, A NATIVE OF PUERTO RICO, WAS A TOOL-AND-DIE WORKER WITH A THIRD-GRADE EDUCATION. WHILE HE SPOKE NO ENGLISH, HE WAS FLUENT IN THE LANGUAGE OF HARD WORK.

EMPIRE
Tool
&
DIE

HER MOTHER, CELINA BÁEZ, WORKED AS A TELEPHONE OPERATOR. SHE LATER BECAME A LICENSED PRACTICAL NURSE.

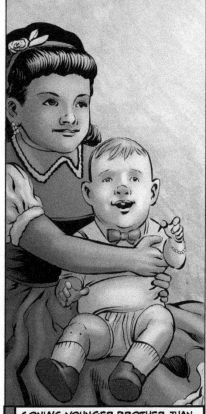

SONIA'S YOUNGER BROTHER JUAN COMPLETED THE FAMILY PORTRAIT IN 1957.

THAT SAME YEAR, THE FAMILY LEFT THEIR CRAMPED TENEMENT FOR COMPARATIVELY SPACIOUS LODGINGS AT THE BRONXDALE HOUSES HOUSING PROJECT. THE NEW DIGS WERE CLEANER, SAFER, AND MORE RACIALLY AND ETHNICALLY DIVERSE.

ALL THINGS CONSIDERED, IT WASN'T SUCH A BAD LIFE. THE CATHOLIC CHURCH SUPPLIED ORDER, RITUAL, AND A SET OF RULES TO LIVE BY.

LIVING IN THE BRONX, SHE NATURALLY BECAME A FAN OF THE NEIGHBORHOOD BASEBALL TEAM, A RAGTAG LITTLE OUTFIT KNOWN AS THE NEW YORK YANKEES.

FOR ENTERTAINMENT, SONIA WENT TO THE MOVIES REGULARLY. ONE OF HER FAVORITE PERFORMERS WAS CANTINFLAS, THE MEXICAN FILM COMEDIAN WHO HAS BEEN CALLED "MEXICO'S ANSWER TO JERRY LEWIS."

AND IN THE SUMMERS, THE FAMILY HEADED OFF TO PUERTO RICO FOR A LITTLE FUN IN THE SUN.

LIFE WASN'T ALL POTATO PANCAKES AND APPLESAUCE OF COURSE. WHEN SHE WAS EIGHT YEARS OLD, SONIA WAS DIAGNOSED WITH JUVENILE DIABETES. SHE STARTED TAKING DAILY INSULIN INJECTIONS.

WHEN SHE WAS NINE, SONIA'S FATHER DIED. IF HAVING TO CHECK HER BLOOD SUGAR THREE TIMES A DAY DIDN'T INSTILL SELF-DISCIPLINE AND INDEPENDENCE, BEING THE OLDEST CHILD OF A SINGLE MOTHER SURE DID.

LUCKILY SONIA WAS AN AVID READER AND COULD FIND TEMPORARY RESPITE FROM HER TROUBLES IN THE ADVENTURES OF THAT PLUCKY "GIRL DETECTIVE," NANCY DREW.

AND OF COURSE THERE WAS ALWAYS TELEVISION—PERRY MASON, TO BE EXACT. IN THE ABSENCE OF HER DAD, RAYMOND BURR'S UNFLAPPABLE TV LAWYER BECAME SONIA'S PRINCIPAL ROLE MODEL.

"I WAS GOING TO COLLEGE AND I WAS GOING TO BECOME AN ATTORNEY," SHE SAID. "I KNEW THAT WHEN I WAS TEN."

ONCE SHE HAD SET HER GOAL, THERE WAS NO STOPPING HER. EVEN MORE IMPORTANTLY, SHE HAD HER MOTHER IN HER CORNER. CELINA SOTOMAYOR MADE A POINT OF BUYING THE FAMILY A COMPLETE SET OF THE ENCYCLOPEDIA BRITANNICA.

ALL THAT SELF-DIRECTED READING PAID OFF. AT THE BLESSED SACRAMENT SCHOOL, SONIA WAS CLASS VALEDICTORIAN AND COMPILED A NEAR-PERFECT ATTENDANCE RECORD.

WHEN SHE WASN'T READING OR STUDYING, SONIA WAS WORKING—IN A LOCAL STORE, AT FIRST, AND LATER AT A HOSPITAL.

ABOUT THE ONLY THING STANDING IN THE WAY OF HIGH ACHIEVEMENT WERE HER SURROUNDINGS. OF LATE, THE ONCE-PRISTINE BRONXDALE HOUSES HAD BECOME A GODFORSAKEN HELLHOLE—RIFE WITH GANGS, JUNKIES, AND PETTY CRIME.

SO IN 1970, WHEN SONIA WAS 16, THE FAMILY PICKED UP AND LEFT, MOVING TO THE CO-OP CITY RESIDENTIAL APARTMENT COMPLEX IN A SAFER, MORE PROSPEROUS PART OF THE BRONX.

SONIA NOW COMMUTED EVERY MORNING TO THE ACADEMICALLY RIGOROUS CARDINAL SPELLMAN HIGH SCHOOL.

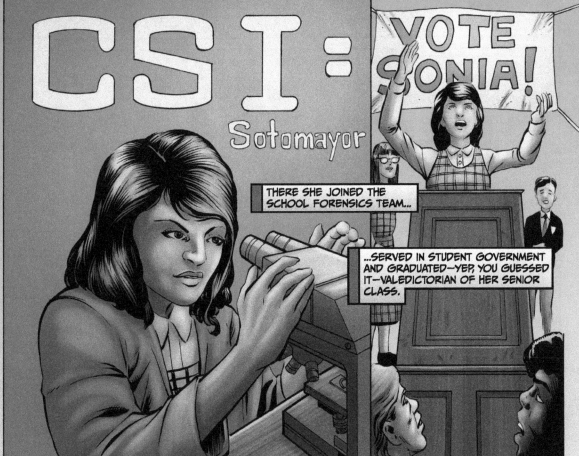

CSI:
Sotomayor

VOTE SONIA!

THERE SHE JOINED THE SCHOOL FORENSICS TEAM...

...SERVED IN STUDENT GOVERNMENT AND GRADUATED—YEP, YOU GUESSED IT—VALEDICTORIAN OF HER SENIOR CLASS.

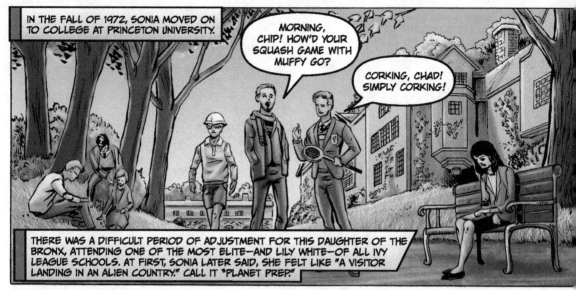

IN THE FALL OF 1972, SONIA MOVED ON TO COLLEGE AT PRINCETON UNIVERSITY.

MORNING, CHIP! HOW'D YOUR SQUASH GAME WITH MUFFY GO?

CORKING, CHAD! SIMPLY CORKING!

THERE WAS A DIFFICULT PERIOD OF ADJUSTMENT FOR THIS DAUGHTER OF THE BRONX, ATTENDING ONE OF THE MOST ELITE—AND LILY WHITE—OF ALL IVY LEAGUE SCHOOLS. AT FIRST, SONIA LATER SAID, SHE FELT LIKE "A VISITOR LANDING IN AN ALIEN COUNTRY." CALL IT "PLANET PREP."

HA HA HA HA HA! RIPPING! VERY WITTY!

AND SO I SAID TO HENRY L. STIMSON, "MR. SECRETARY, IF YOU RUN THIS COUNTRY'S FOREIGN POLICY ANYTHING LIKE YOU STEER THIS YACHT...

...WE SHALL ALL BE VOTING FOR ROOSEVELT IN THE NEXT ELECTION!"

FOR HER ENTIRE FRESHMAN YEAR, SHE WAS TOO INTIMIDATED TO SPEAK UP IN CLASS.

IN TIME, SONIA WAS ABLE TO OVERCOME HER CLASS ANXIETY.

DETERMINED TO IMPROVE HER LANGUAGE SKILLS, SHE PUT IN LONG HOURS AT THE LIBRARY STUDYING THE CLASSICS.

BY GEORGE, YOU'VE GOT IT!

SHE WORKED WITH A PROFESSOR OUTSIDE OF CLASS TO INCREASE HER KNOWLEDGE BASE AND IMPROVE HER POISE AND CONFIDENCE.

AND SHE NEVER LOST TOUCH WITH HER HERITAGE. SHE DEVOTED HER SENIOR THESIS TO THE TOPIC OF PUERTO RICO'S STRUGGLE FOR INDEPENDENCE UNDER THE LEADERSHIP OF LUIS MUÑOZ MARÍN.

SHE BECAME ACTIVE IN CAMPUS POLITICS, RALLYING PRINCETON'S LATINO COMMUNITY ON BEHALF OF PUERTO RICAN STUDENT RECRUITMENT AND FACULTY HIRING.

OFF-CAMPUS, SHE SPENT HER TIME VOLUNTEERING WITH LATINO PATIENTS AT THE TRENTON PSYCHIATRIC HOSPITAL.

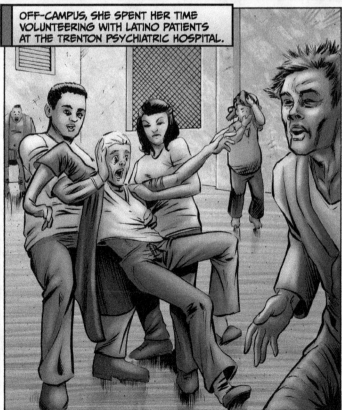

IT WAS THE HARDEST FOUR YEARS OF HER LIFE THUS FAR, BUT SONIA GRADUATED SUMMA CUM LAUDE IN 1976. AN IVY LEAGUE DEGREE WAS HERS AT LAST.

BUT GRADUATING FROM COLLEGE WASN'T SONIA'S ONLY REASON FOR CELEBRATING. THAT SUMMER, SHE MARRIED LONGTIME BOYFRIEND KEVIN EDWARD NOONAN. SHE NOW STYLED HERSELF SONIA SOTOMAYOR DE NOONAN.

AND WHEN THE PARTY ENDED, SHE GOT RIGHT BACK TO BUSINESS. SHE ENROLLED IN YALE LAW SCHOOL, WHERE SHE BECAME AN EDITOR ON THE PRESTIGIOUS LAW JOURNAL.

AFTER SECURING HER LAW DEGREE IN 1979, SONIA WAS QUICKLY SCOOPED UP BY FAMED MANHATTAN DISTRICT ATTORNEY ROBERT MORGENTHAU, WHO HAD A REPUTATION FOR HIRING ONLY THE BEST, MOST QUALIFIED LAWYERS IN THE COUNTRY.

IT WAS THE BEST TRAINING GROUND A YOUNG LAWYER COULD ASK FOR. UNDER MORGENTHAU'S GUIDANCE, SONIA PROSECUTED EVERYTHING FROM SHOPLIFTING AND PROSTITUTION CASES TO MURDERS, ASSAULTS, AND ROBBERIES.

IN HER HIGHEST PROFILE CASE, SONIA HELPED CONVICT THE SO-CALLED "TARZAN MURDERER"— A LUNATIC WHO KILLED PEOPLE AFTER SWINGING INTO THEIR APARTMENT WINDOWS.

MORGENTHAU EFFUSIVELY SANG HER PRAISES, CALLING HER A "FEARLESS AND EFFECTIVE PROSECUTOR."

AFTER A WHILE, HOWEVER, THE HIGH-PRESSURE JOB TOOK ITS TOLL. BURNED OUT, SHE LEFT THE D.A.'S OFFICE IN 1983. "AFTER A WHILE, YOU FORGET THERE ARE DECENT, LAW-ABIDING PEOPLE IN LIFE," SONIA SAID LATER.

ANOTHER CASUALTY OF THE JOB WAS HER MARRIAGE TO KEVIN EDWARD NOONAN. THEY DIVORCED THAT SAME YEAR.

FLUSSSHHH!

IN 1984, SONIA WENT INTO PRIVATE PRACTICE WITH A CORPORATE LAW FIRM.

HERE'S YOUR PAYCHECK, SONIA. WELCOME TO THE FIRM!

GA-GA-GA-GOING!!!

ATTORNEY SONIA SOTOMA

IT WAS A CHANCE FOR HER TO TRY AND ARGUE MORE CASES IN COURT—AND TO MAKE SOME REAL CHEDDAR FOR THE FIRST TIME IN HER LIFE.

MANY OF HER CLIENTS WERE INTERNATIONAL CORPORATIONS DOING BUSINESS IN THE UNITED STATES. SHE SPENT MOST OF HER TIME TRACKING DOWN AND SUING PEOPLE WHO SOLD COUNTERFEIT LUXURY HANDBAGS.

AFTER ONE SUCH CASE, SONIA TOOK PART IN A RITUAL CRUSHING BY GARBAGE TRUCK OF 9000 ERSATZ FENDI HANDBAGS STAGED AT NEW YORK CITY'S TAVERN ON THE GREEN RESTAURANT.

AFTER TWO YEARS OF CHASING HANDBAG BANDITS, HOWEVER, SONIA ONCE AGAIN GREW BORED WITH HER JOB.

IN 1986, SHE APPEARED ON THE ABC MORNING SHOW GOOD MORNING AMERICA, WHERE SHE COMPLAINED THAT THE VAST MAJORITY OF THE WORK SHE HAD DONE SINCE LAW SCHOOL WAS PURE DRUDGERY.

IT WAS TIME FOR ANOTHER CAREER CHANGE. IN 1988, SHE ACCEPTED AN OFFER FROM NEW YORK CITY MAYOR ED KOCH TO SERVE ON THE CITY'S NEWLY FORMED CAMPAIGN FINANCE BOARD. SHE REMAINED IN THAT JOB FOR THE NEXT FOUR YEARS.

HOW'M I DOIN'?

IF I AM RE-ELECTED, I WILL MAKE SURE WE GET A LATINO JUDGE ON THE U.S. DISTRICT COURT..

MEANWHILE, NEW YORK'S SENIOR U.S. SENATOR, DANIEL PATRICK MOYNIHAN, WAS SEARCHING AROUND FOR A QUALIFIED HISPANIC TO ELEVATE TO THE POSITION OF DISTRICT COURT JUDGE.

AFTER HIS RE-ELECTION, A MEMBER OF MOYNIHAN'S STAFF CAME TO HIM WITH THE FOLLOWING RECOMMENDATION.

HAVE WE GOT A JUDGE FOR YOU!

WITH THE HELP OF HIS GOP COUNTERPART, ALPHONSE D'AMATO (WHO HAD AGREED TO SIGN OFF ON ALL JUDICIAL RECOMMENDATIONS), MOYNIHAN GOT SONIA APPOINTED TO THE BENCH BY REPUBLICAN PRESIDENT GEORGE H.W. BUSH.

WITH ONE STROKE OF A PEN, SONIA SOTOMAYOR BECAME THE YOUNGEST JUDGE IN THE SOUTHERN DISTRICT, THE FIRST HISPANIC FEDERAL JUDGE IN NEW YORK STATE, AND THE FIRST PUERTO RICAN WOMAN TO SERVE AS A JUDGE ON A U.S. FEDERAL COURT.

GREAT CHOICE, FELLAS! NOW...WHO'S FOR PORK RINDS?

SHE DEVELOPED A REPUTATION AS A TOUGH-AS-NAILS, PRO-PROSECUTION JUDGE KNOWN FOR DOLING OUT STIFF SENTENCES.

HANG 'IM HIGH, BOYS! HANG 'IM HIGH!

CIVIL CASES CAME BEFORE HER AS WELL. IN 1995, SHE ISSUED THE INJUNCTION THAT ENDED THE 232-DAY LONG MAJOR LEAGUE BASEBALL STRIKE.

IT'S GREAT TO BE "PLAYING BALL" ONCE AGAIN, EH, JUDGE SOTOMAYOR?

YOU GOT THAT RIGHT, COMMISSIONER ALLAN "BUD" SELIG!

THAT SAME YEAR, SHE RULED AGAINST THE AUTHOR OF A BOOK OF *SEINFELD* TV TRIVIA, CITING INFRINGEMENT OF COPYRIGHT AGAINST THE SHOW'S CREATORS.

SHE EVEN DEFIED THE WHITE HOUSE WHEN SHE ISSUED A RULING ALLOWING THE *WALL STREET JOURNAL* TO PUBLISH THE SUICIDE NOTE OF FORMER DEPUTY WHITE HOUSE COUNSEL VINCE FOSTER.

Vince Foster

IN 1997, FOSTER'S FORMER BOSS, PRESIDENT BILL CLINTON, REWARDED SONIA FOR HER EVEN-HANDED JUDGMENT BY NOMINATING HER TO THE U.S. COURT OF APPEALS FOR THE SECOND CIRCUIT.

CONGRATULATIONS, JUDGE! HAVE A CIGAR?

OVER THE NEXT DECADE, SHE WOULD HEAR APPEALS IN MORE THAN 3,000 CASES AND WRITE MORE THAN 380 OPINIONS.

SHE GAINED A REPUTATION FOR RUNNING A "HOT BENCH"— LEGALSPEAK FOR ASKING TOUGH, SOMETIMES BELLIGERENT QUESTIONS OF LAWYERS WHO ARGUED CASES BEFORE HER.

SHE ALSO FOUND HERSELF IN HIGH DEMAND ON THE PUBLIC SPEAKING CIRCUIT. SHE APPEARED FREQUENTLY BEFORE GROUPS OF HISPANIC LAW SCHOOL STUDENTS.

EVERY NIGHT SHE RETURNED TO THE TASTEFULLY DECORATED HOME SHE HAD PURCHASED IN NEW YORK CITY'S GREENWICH VILLAGE. SHE LIVED MODESTLY, FOR SOMEONE OF SUCH IMMENSE POWER AND INFLUENCE.

SHE STILL HAD TO GIVE HERSELF DAILY INSULIN INJECTIONS, A REGULAR REMINDER THAT DIABETES CAN BE CONTROLLED, BUT NEVER CURED.

AS FOR ROMANCE...AS THEY SAY IN NEW YORK: FUGGEDABOUTIT. HER WORK ON THE COURT OF APPEALS CONSUMED NEARLY ALL OF HER TIME. "I HAVE FOUND IT DIFFICULT TO MAINTAIN A RELATIONSHIP WHILE I'VE PURSUED MY CAREER," SHE ADMITTED.

SHE WAS BRIEFLY ENGAGED TO A NEW YORK CONSTRUCTION MAGNATE, PETER WHITE, BUT THEIR RELATIONSHIP ENDED IN 2000, BEFORE THEY TIED THE KNOT. SONIA WAS REDUCED TO EATING TAKEOUT FOOD AND BURYING HERSELF IN HER WORK ONCE MORE.

JUST ABOUT THE MOST THRILLING THING THAT HAPPENED TO HER IN THIS PERIOD OCCURRED IN NOVEMBER OF 2008, WHEN SHE WON $8,283 PLAYING THE SLOTS AT A LOCAL CASINO.

AWWWW YYYEAAAHH!

JUDGE SONIA NEEDS A NEW SET OF ROBES!

GENERAL TSO'S CHICKEN! THIS ISN'T WHAT I ORDERED! WHERE'S MY MOO GOO GAI PAN?

LUCKY FOR SONIA, SOMEONE ELSE HIT THE JACKPOT THAT MONTH AS WELL. BARACK HUSSEIN OBAMA WAS ELECTED PRESIDENT OF THE UNITED STATES.

SONIA MAY NOT HAVE KNOWN IT YET, BUT THE GRAY, LONELY LIFE OF AN OBSCURE APPELLATE JUDGE WAS ABOUT TO COME TO AN END FOR HER...FOR GOOD!

ON MAY 26, 2009, PRESIDENT OBAMA NOMINATED SONIA TO REPLACE THE RETIRING JUSTICE DAVID SOUTER ON THE U.S. SUPREME COURT. SHE WOULD BE ONLY THE THIRD WOMAN AND THE FIRST HISPANIC TO SERVE ON THE HIGH COURT.

SONIA, WHAT YOU'VE SHOWN IN YOUR LIFE IS THAT IT DOESN'T MATTER WHERE YOU COME FROM, WHAT YOU LOOK LIKE, OR WHAT CHALLENGES LIFE THROWS YOUR WAY -- NO DREAM IS BEYOND REACH IN THE UNITED STATES OF AMERICA!

ALMOST IMMEDIATELY, THE MEDIA AND CONSERVATIVE CRITICS SEIZED ON COMMENTS SONIA HAD MADE DURING AN ADDRESS TO HISPANIC LAW STUDENTS AT THE UNIVERSITY OF CALIFORNIA AT BERKELEY SEVERAL YEARS BEFORE.

I WOULD HOPE THAT A WISE LATINA WOMAN WITH THE RICHNESS OF HER EXPERIENCES WOULD MORE OFTEN THAN NOT REACH A BETTER CONCLUSION THAN A WHITE MALE WHO HASN'T LIVED THAT LIFE.

AND THERE WAS A WHOLE SEPARATE KERFUFFLE OVER A RULING SHE HAD ISSUED IN A DISCRIMINATION CASE INVOLVING A GROUP OF DISGRUNTLED WHITE NEW HAVEN FIREFIGHTERS.

WITHIN DAYS, SONIA WAS BEING DENOUNCED AS A RACIST.

ONE RIGHT-WING FORMER CONGRESSMAN EVEN ATTACKED HER MEMBERSHIP IN THE MAINSTREAM HISPANIC CIVIL RIGHTS ORGANIZATION, LA RAZA.

LA RAZA IS NOTHING MORE THAN A LATINO KKK WITHOUT THE HOODS OR THE NOOSES!

msnbc

RUSH LIMBAUGH ATTACKED HER ON THE RADIO...

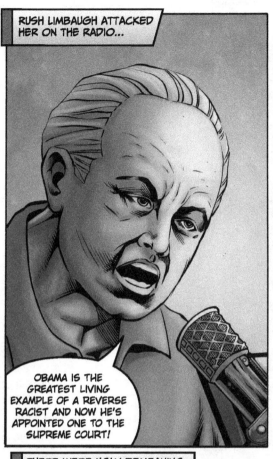

OBAMA IS THE GREATEST LIVING EXAMPLE OF A REVERSE RACIST AND NOW HE'S APPOINTED ONE TO THE SUPREME COURT!

NEWT GINGRICH SAVAGED HER ON TWITTER.

WHITE MAN RACIST NOMINEE WOULD BE FORCED TO WITHDRAW. LATINA WOMAN RACIST SHOULD ALSO WITHDRAW.

THERE WERE UGLY, DEMEANING IMAGES OF HER CIRCULATED ON THE INTERNET.

FOR HER PART, SONIA KEPT HER HEAD UP, AND SIMPLY WENT ABOUT THE BUSINESS OF MEETING THE SENATORS WHO WOULD VOTE ON HER NOMINATION, TO SHARE WITH THEM HER JUDICIAL PHILOSOPHY.

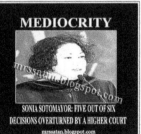

WHICH WAS KIND OF HARD TO DO, CONSIDERING SHE HAD RECENTLY BROKEN HER ANKLE WHILE RUNNING TO CATCH A PLANE AT THE AIRPORT.

WHEN THE SENATE JUDICIARY COMMITTEE HEARING ON HER NOMINATION CAME TO ORDER ON JULY 13TH, SONIA WAS BACK ON HER FEET—AND FIGHTING BACK AGAINST CHARGES THAT SHE PUT HER SYMPATHY FOR CERTAIN ETHNIC GROUPS ABOVE THE LAW.

I DO NOT BELIEVE THAT ANY ETHNIC, RACIAL OR GENDER GROUP HAS AN ADVANTAGE IN SOUND JUDGMENT.

SHE FACED TOUGH QUESTIONS FROM REPUBLICANS ABOUT HER REPUTATION FOR ASKING TOUGH QUESTIONS OF THE LAWYERS WHO ARGUED BEFORE HER.

DO YOU THINK YOU HAVE A TEMPERAMENT PROBLEM?

IN THE END, SHE PREVAILED BY A 13-6 VOTE OF THE JUDICIARY COMMITTEE. THE FULL SENATE WOULD VOTE TO CONFIRM HER ON AUGUST 6, 2009

ALL THAT LAY AHEAD NOW WAS THE ARRIVAL OF FALL— AND A CHANCE FOR JUDGE SOTOMAYOR TO TAKE HER RIGHTFUL PLACE ON AMERICA'S HIGHEST COURT.

I KNOW ONE THING...YOU CAN BET YOUR BOTTOM DOLLAR THOSE SUPREME COURT GET-TOGETHERS ARE GOING TO BE A WHOLE LOT MORE INTERESTING FROM NOW ON!

WELCOME, JUSTICE SOTOMAYOR!

Darren G. Davis
Publisher

Jason Schultz
Vice President

Jackie Stickley
New Business Development

Jarred Weisfeld
Literary Manager

Kailey Marsh
Entertainment Manager

Warren Montgomery
Coordinator

Nikki Borror
Coordinator

Maggie Jessup
Publicity

www.bluewaterprod.com

CPSIA information can be obtained
at www.ICGtesting.com
Printed in the USA
BVHW011155070421
604420BV00010B/53